Enchanting
THAILAND

MICK SHIPPEN

JOHN BEAUFOY PUBLISHING

Contents

Top left: *Wat Jong Kham and Wat Jong Klang temples are located beside the lake in the centre of Mae Hong Son, northern Thailand.*

Top right: *A highlight of Mae Hong Son's cultural calendar is the Shan ordination ceremony known as Poi Sang Long.*

Above: *A glittering Buddha image caught in the half light at a temple in Ayutthaya.*

Chapter 1: A Land of Intrigue and Adventure

A country of intrigue and adventure, Thailand's exotic mix of glistening temples, extraordinary annual festivals, idyllic tropical islands and genuinely hospitable people has made it one of the world's most popular and rewarding tourist destinations. The country is home to a distinctive culture that enables old traditions to sit comfortably within a prosperous and progressive society, and which enriches the lives of all who visit.

One of the original 'Asian tiger economies', over the past two decades Thailand has survived boom and bust, undergone recovery and experienced political upheaval, yet, despite this turbulence, it still welcomes all travellers with a warm and gracious smile. Most visits to the country begin and end in Bangkok, a cosmopolitan and bustling metropolis of over ten million citizens. A city of contrasts, here ostentatious mega malls and towering skyscrapers overshadow serene temples and vibrant local markets, motorcycle taxis whisk businessmen to modern SkyTrain and underground stations, ferries carry them across the Chao Phraya River and chic restaurants compete for custom with delicious street-side dining. And then, of course, there's the notorious risqué nightlife at the infamous Patpong, Soi Cowboy and Nana Plaza. Big, bold and brash, Bangkok is truly a city that never sleeps.

Top: Although Thailand is developing extremely quickly, beneath the brash modern exterior and traffic-clogged streets there are pockets of calm and tranquillity that reveal the more spiritual side of Thai people.

Left: Thai temple architecture is extremely ornate and colourful. Even new temples built with the donations of worshippers still adhere to the forms and conventions of the past.

Rich Cultural Heritage

The northeast of Thailand, a group of 18 culturally diverse provinces collectively known as Issan, is one of the country's most fascinating, but little visited, regions. Here, travellers can discover ancient ruins such as Phimai, a temple structure that predates Angkor in Cambodia, and Khao Yai National Park, a haven for endangered wildlife. The north attracts adventure tourists and nature lovers who after a few days exploring the city of Chiang Mai head to the mountains and perhaps trek through inspiring scenery to gain insight into unique hill tribe cultures, go white-water rafting or enjoy more leisurely pursuits such as bird watching. Central Thailand contains the fascinating UNESCO World Heritage Site of Ayutthaya and paradise awaits travellers in the south where luxurious resorts and spas overlook the pristine white sand beaches and the crystal clear waters of the Andaman Sea.

Whether experiencing the vibrancy and creative energy of bustling Bangkok, exploring the rural heartlands of the northeast, discovering the hill tribes of the mountainous north, or simply lazing on a beach down south, the sheer variety of sights and sounds in enchanting Thailand are capable of creating memories to last a lifetime.

Above: Many temples feature enormous Buddha images that are an attraction for worshippers from all over the country who come to make merit by offering donations. The image pictured here is of a 19-m (62-ft) high Buddha at Wat Phanan Choeng in Ayutthaya.

Left: At the Poi Sang Long ordination ceremony boys entering the monkhood have their heads shaved and are dressed in beautiful costumes before being paraded through the town.

Geography & Climate

Situated in the heart of Southeast Asia, Thailand encompasses an area of 513,115 km² (198,129 sq miles), bordering Laos to the north and east, Myanmar to the west, Cambodia to the east, and Malaysia to the south.

Thailand is divided into four main regions with a total of 77 provinces. The central plains are comprised of 24 provinces. A network of rivers and canals makes this the most fertile part of Thailand, supporting vast fields of rice, sugar palm plantations and a variety of fruits. In the northeast, commonly known as Issan, both Lao and Khmer influences can be seen and felt within the ancient temple ruins, and in the distinctive cuisine and the region's dialect.

The mountainous north is home to Thailand's hill tribe population. The region is also renowned for its unique

Above: Although many in Thailand's south are involved in the tourist industry, communities of fishermen who make their living from the sea still exist.

Left: Northern Thailand is known as the garden of the country and produces a wide variety of fruits and vegetables on the slopes of deforested hillsides.

Lanna cultural traditions and architecture that includes some of the country's most majestic temples.

Bound by the Gulf of Thailand and the Andaman Sea, the south is a beach paradise with beautiful islands scattered off the coast attracting visitors from around the world.

Thailand benefits from a tropical climate with average high temperatures of 35 °C (95 °F). There are three overlapping seasons; the monsoon lasts from May to October, when it turns moderate to cool until February. Temperatures and humidity then begin rise throughout the hot season, peaking in April.

Above left: Promthep Cape on the island of Phuket is a popular location to enjoy fabulous sunsets. Located at the southernmost tip of the island, the viewpoint on the rocky cape is fringed by tall, elegantly proportioned sugar palms.

Above right: Orchids are grown commercially in the north but the forests are also the habitat of rare wild species.

Right: Much of rural Thailand's central plains and the northeast are given over to rice paddies.

A Brief History of Thailand

Thailand has a long and fascinating history. Archaeological excavations in the northeast indicate that there were people living in the area over 2,000 years ago. The most famous discovery in recent years was the prehistoric find at Ban Chiang. Here, during the mid-1960s, a wide range of earthenware pots were discovered, the earliest believed to date from 2100 BC while production continued up until AD 200. Other archaeological sites of significance have been unearthed at Baan Prasat near Khorat in northeastern Thailand and Baan Koh Noi near Sukhothai.

By the 6th century Dvaravati period, thriving agricultural communities had been established as far north as Lamphun and south to Pattani. The collection of city states lasted until the 11th century when it quickly declined under the political domination of Khmer invaders.

Thailand's Sukhothai period from 1238 to 1438 is regarded as the beginning of Thai history. At its height, the kingdom is thought to have wielded dominance from Nakhon Si Thammarat in the south, to Luang Prabang in northern Laos, and Martaban in Myanmar. Sukhothai is considered by historians to be the first true Thai kingdom and, with nine kings ruling over two centuries, a stable period of history. King Ramkhamhaeng, the second king, established a system of writing which became the basis for the modern Thai script. The king also promoted Buddhism which gave birth to classic forms of Thai religious art.

The production of glazed ceramic wares was extremely important to the economy of Sukhothai. Pots from the many kilns just outside the city and in nearby Sri Satchanalai were exported all over the region. To this day, sunken trade vessels in the Gulf of Thailand and in Malaysian waters continue to be discovered by marine archaeologists and reveal yet more secrets from the Sukhothai period.

Above right: Elephant imagery was commonly used in Sukhothai period religious architecture. This picture shows one of 24 elephants that surround the 'chedi' at Wat Sorasak, a 15th-century temple just north of the old city.

Right: Wat Phra That Lampang Luang is said to be the oldest wooden temple in Thailand, dating back to 1476. Inside, wooden panels depict scenes from the Buddhist scriptures and show foreigners being welcomed.

Left: The Sukhothai Historical Park covers a vast area and is best explored by bicycle. The central area is surrounded by a moat and features 21 magnificent temples.

Below: In Chiang Rai, a bronze statue has been erected to honour King Mengrai (1259–1317).

Rise & Fall of Ayutthaya

Following the death of King Ramkhamhaeng, Sukhothai's influence began to decrease. With the demise of King Thammaracha in 1438, the last king of Sukhothai, the kingdom became a province within the now dominant kingdom of Ayutthaya.

During the 14th and 15th centuries, Ayutthaya became increasingly powerful and its rule began to expand its reach eastward to include Angkor in Cambodia. By the mid-16th century Ayutthaya was sacked by an invading Burmese army and, along with Lanna in north Thailand, came under their control. Although Thais regained both areas by the end of the century, Burma invaded Ayutthaya again in 1767, winning a fierce two-year battle. During this time large numbers of Ayutthaya's manuscripts, religious sculptures and temples were destroyed.

New Capital in Thonburi

In 1769, after the fall of Ayutthaya, a new Thai capital was established at Thonburi. Set on the banks of the Chao Phraya River opposite present-day Bangkok, Thonburi was ruled over by King Thaksin. With the kingdom still in turmoil, Thonburi remained the capital for just 15 years, collapsing because of disorder at the end of his reign.

Below left: After Sukhothai, Ayutthaya is considered Thailand's next most important historical site. Built in 1357, Wat Yai Chai Mongkhon features an enormous 'chedi' and Buddha images.

Below: Even though the temples fell into disrepair centuries ago, the Buddha images are still revered, being regularly draped in yellow robes and given offerings of incense and flowers by worshippers.

Ratanakosin Period to the Present Day

In 1782 King Rama I was crowned. As the first king of the Chakri dynasty, he promptly moved the capital across the river to Bangkok. In 1809 Rama II, son of Rama I, took the throne and ruled until 1824. King Rama III (ruled 1824–51) began to develop trade with China and increase domestic agricultural production.

King Mongkut, Rama IV took the throne in 1851 and quickly established diplomatic relations with European nations and used his skill to avoid colonization. He also began a period of trade reform and modernization of the Thai education system. His son, King Chulalongkorn, Rama V (ruled 1868–1910), continued this tradition with

the modernization of the legal and administrative systems, and the construction of railways. During his 15-year reign from 1910 to 1925 King Vajiravudha (Rama VI) introduced compulsory education and other reforms.

In 1925 the brother of King Vajiravudha, King Prajadhipok Rama VII (1925–1935) ascended the throne. Seven years later, a group of soldiers and civil servants mounted a bloodless coup d'état which led to the establishment of a constitutional monarchy. A key military leader, Phibul Songkhram, took power and maintained control until after the end of the Second World War. Rama VIII, Ananda Mahidol, became king in 1935 but was assassinated in mysterious circumstances in 1946. He was succeeded by his younger brother, Bhumibol Adulyadej, Rama IX. In the same year, under Rama IX's reign, the country's name was officially changed from Siam to Thailand or in the Thai language, *prathet Thai*, literally 'land of the free'.

His Majesty King Bhumibol Adulyadej, Rama IX remains on the throne today. Highly revered by the Thai people, he is the world's longest reigning monarch.

Left: *Thailand's king is deeply revered and his image is to be seen everywhere.*

Above: *In central Bangkok a road has been named to proclaim the people's feeling for the king.*

The People

O ne of Thailand's greatest assets is its people. Thais are genuinely warm, friendly and their natural hospitality welcomes all nationalities and religions with an open heart, making visitors feel well appreciated and at home.

Thailand is a diverse country with a population comprised of many different races and ethnicities. Making up 75 per cent of the population of around 67,500,000 citizens (2011), Thais are the majority, and are part of a larger Tai ethno-linguistic community which is also present in neighbouring Southeast Asian countries.

Above: The majority of Thais are Buddhist and regularly visit the temple of a shrine to make merit.

Top: Monks at Thai temples may preach non-attachment, but they are switched on to the internet and many have active websites to help reach their followers.

Thailand has a long history of Chinese immigration and the present-day Chinese population is thought to be over 15 per cent, many of whom are Teochew from the Guangdong region of China. Today, Thailand's Chinese population dominates commerce and politics. In the north, hill tribes including the Akha, Hmong, Karen, Lisu and Lahu migrated from Tibet, Myanmar, China and Laos over the past 200 years and today comprise 8 per cent of the population while ethnic Malays in the south make up just 3 per cent.

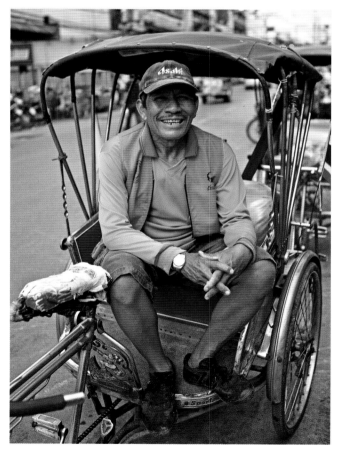

Above left: In the north, the population includes several ethnic hill tribes.

Above right: Many towns have a minority of Muslims but most are in the southern provinces bordering Malaysia.

Right: The majority of Thais working in the service industries come from the northeast.

Religion

Once referred to by early travellers as the Land of the Yellow Robes, Thailand's population is 95 per cent Buddhist and it is the only country in the world where the constitution stipulates that the monarch must be Buddhist.

Buddhism is first thought to have arrived in Thailand as far back as the 3rd century but it was in the 13th century Sukhothai period that monks from Sri Lanka introduced Theravada Buddhism. Spreading throughout the country, it soon became the dominant religion. In Thai society, Buddhism has strongly influenced art, architecture and literature, and inspires the tolerant nature of the Thai people.

Top right: *A young man in a moment of contemplation before his ordination.*

Above: *A woman praying before offering flowers and incense to an image of Buddha.*

Above: *On special religious days, thousands of worshippers will go to the temple.*

Diversity & Tolerance

Islam, Christianity, Hinduism and animism are also present in Thailand. Long before Buddhism took root in the country, the people turned to the spirit world for guidance and protection. Today, many of the hill tribes in the north still practise animism, although some have been dominated by missionaries and converted to Christianity. The far southern Thai provinces of Yala, Pattani and Narathiwat are populated by ethnic Malay Muslims. However, in the past Muslims have also migrated to Thailand from China, Iran, Pakistan and Indonesia. Today, there are significant Thai Muslim communities living in Ayutthaya, Bangkok, Nakhon Nayok and Nonthaburi.

Right: Religious tattoos are common in Thailand. For those women who don't want to mark their skin permanently, monks will also create them using holy oil, as here.

Below: A man closely examines a Buddha amulet. Believed to offer the wearer protection, the trade in amulets is a multi-million baht business.

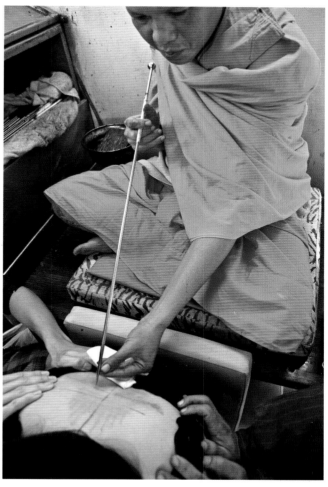

Superstition & Animism

Thai people are extremely superstitious, turning to fortune tellers for insight into their lives, amulets and tattoos for protection and the spirit world for good luck.

Thai Buddhism borrows strongly from animism and there are many colourful spirit houses erected outside homes and businesses. The purpose of these beautiful miniature homes is to provide a residence for the spirits when the land that they reside on has been disturbed by construction. From small and simple to positively palatial, spirit houses, Thai and Chinese, are one of the most noticeable cultural curiosities in Thailand. Offerings of food, water, flowers and incense are made at spirit houses each day to placate any mischievous spirits.

Thai Food – The Spice of Life

Thailand has often been described as a 'food culture', a statement that implies that food is more than simply sustenance but central to almost every aspect of the social life. Indeed, one only needs to wander around any town to realize just how true that statement is.

The availability of food and the mind-boggling range of dishes on offer make Thailand one of the most exciting places in the world to dine.

A frequently heard greeting in the country is '*kin khao yang?*', or 'have you eaten yet?' Dining for Thai people is a relaxed affair, a time to sit together and chat and share a wonderful array of food.

Rice

Rice is the staple of Thailand; a grain that has shaped the landscape and defined the culture. Served at every meal, the preferred choice is jasmine rice, also known as fragrant rice due to its pleasant aroma. In the north and northeast sticky rice or *khao neow* is more popular. Sticky rice also features in a number of desserts and many sweets are made using rice flour.

Above: Thailand is still very much an agrarian nation and produces a huge amount of rice for domestic and international consumption. Many migrant workers in Bangkok will go back home to the provinces at planting and harvest time.

Right: Evening markets, like this one in the Chang Peuk district of Chiang Mai, offer a huge variety of ready-made food to take home and enjoy. Dining street-side at food stalls is also part of Thai life.

Regional Cuisine

Thai cuisine comprises dishes from four distinct regions: the central plains, the north, the northeast and the south. The unifying factor is the way each skillfully combines the elements of spicy, sour, sweet and salty. Key ingredients include the ubiquitous chilli. Fresh, dried, ground or pickled, the chilli is used to add fire to almost every main dish. Lime juice and tamarind provide the sour taste while sweetness comes from palm sugar. The salty taste is added by fish sauce, known as *nam pla*. Made by a process of prolonged salting and fermentation, fish sauce is an essential in almost all dishes and is also sprinkled over food when extra saltiness is required.

Top, centre and above: *Chillies, fresh and dried, are an essential ingredient of almost all Thai dishes. Fish sauce is also found in every dish and is used as a condiment along with sugar and vinegar.*

Eating Thai Style

Dining Thai-style is a lesson in the art of sharing; a fact that undoubtedly adds to the convivial atmosphere of dining with Thai people. Several dishes are ordered, all of which arrive at the table at the same time. A meal may include a spicy salad, fragrant curry, sour and spicy soup, a grilled or steamed fish dish, vegetables and some titbits. All diners tuck into the food together, taking small amounts to their plate of rice as required. Thais eat using a spoon and fork, with chopsticks reserved for Chinese-style noodle dishes.

Below: Thais are enthusiastic eaters, but food must be shared and meals are a leisurely experience. A group of diners will order several dishes, accompanied by rice, and tuck in together.

Street Eats

An essential ingredient that adds undeniable spice to Thai life is the country's stunning variety of street food. Across the country, enterprising vendors have established regular pavement pitches. Many specialize in one particular dish, while others are able to turn their hand to a bewildering selection of enticing cuisine. Yet they all have one thing in common; the food they serve is cheap, tasty and ready in minutes, the very definition of fast food. Whether you are looking for a quick *al fresco* breakfast, a full-blown lunch, a tempting in-between meals nibble or a late night treat, the street vendors have it all, 24 hours a day. Dining street-side in Thailand is a culinary adventure, a feast for the eyes as much as it is for the stomach, and an essential part of any visit to the country.

Left: Thanks to an army of street vendors, it is possible to eat almost anywhere, 24 hours a day.

Below left: Chillies are roasted and pounded together with shallots and garlic to make a spicy dip.

Below: The pungent durian is considered the king of fruits in Thailand but many westerners find it an acquired taste.

Festivals & Celebrations

Thailand is renowned for its wonderful festivals and exciting cultural events that are held throughout the year.

Chinese New Year

Every January or February, the huge Chinese community welcomes the New Year with dancing lions, firecrackers and feasts. Temples in Bangkok's Chinatown teem with worshippers making merit (doing good deeds) and wishing for good fortune during the coming year.

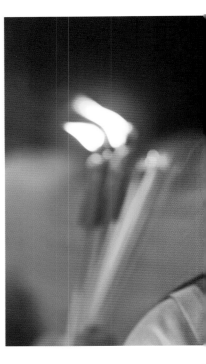

Below: *At Chinese New Year, Bangkok's Yaowarat district teems with members of the city's huge Thai-Chinese community as they celebrate and dine in the street.*

Left: *A young woman lights candles and incense at a shrine in the heart of Chinatown. Throughout the day and night, thousands of people will visit the temples in Yaowarat.*

Below: *In the northern town of Chiang Mai where one of the country's biggest of the Loy Kratong celebrations takes place, thousands of floating lanterns are released into the night sky.*

Loy Kratong

Loy Kratong is one of the most popular festivals in Thailand. It takes place on the night of the full moon in November. In the evening, thousands of people go down to the nearest river to float their *kratong*, a small raft made from a banana palm and decorated with flowers, a candle and incense.

Khao Phansa

Khao Phansa or Buddhist Lent marks the beginning of the rainy season retreat, a three-month period when monks stay within the confines of the temples and devote themselves to study and meditation. The first and last days of this period are marked with candlelit processions.

Poi Sang Long – Festival of Precious Gems

In late March or early April, Poi Sang Long takes place in towns and villages all over Mae Hong Son Province. The Buddhist ordination ceremony is part of the Shan or Tai Yai tradition and was brought to Thailand by settlers from neighbouring Myanmar.

During the event known as the Festival of Precious Gems, young boys are ordained as novices and spend time studying Buddhist doctrine. A colourful spectacle to witness, it is one of the most delightful festivals in the country. On the first day of the four-day ceremony, the boys have their hair shaved off at the temple and are then bathed and anointed with consecrated waters. The following day they are dressed in brightly coloured clothes and paraded through the town as *sang long* – precious gems.

Opposite: The festival is of great importance to the families of the boys and the proud parents help to get them ready for the ceremony and colourful parade that follows.

Below: A boy's mother applies his lipstick in preparation for his ordination. As many as 50 boys in one community may take part in the ceremony.

Above: Shaved and dressed up, a young Shan boy waits to take part in a procession at the Poi Sang Long festival.

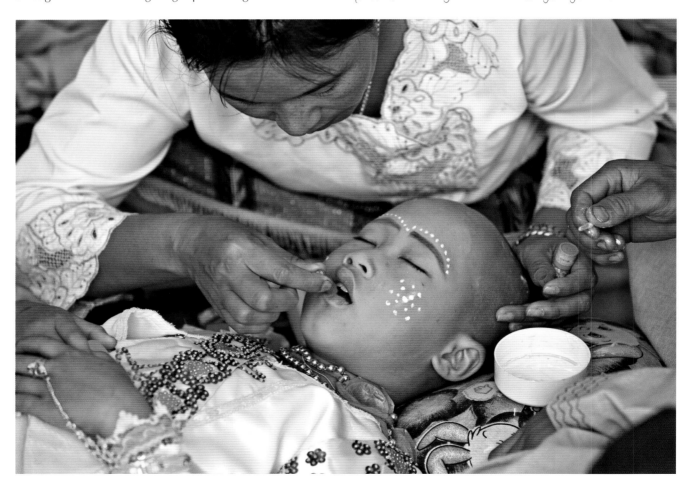

Songkran

A highlight of the annual cultural calendar is Songkran, the Thai New Year. It is one of the most spectacular festivals in the Thai calendar. Today, the national holiday is held across a period of several days, with Songkran Day being marked on 13 April.

The festival takes place at the height of the hot season and acts as a welcome pressure valve for a heat-stressed population. The annual holiday sees a mass exodus from Bangkok as hundreds of thousands of migrant workers travel back to rural areas to visit family and take part in riotous celebrations, parties and the world's biggest water fight! In the north of Thailand paper lanterns known as *khom loy* are released into the night sky.

Above: Although the Thai government likes to promote Songkran as a genteel festival, in truth it is simply a riotous water fight, lasting from dawn to dusk for several days.

Above right: If you don't want to get wet, don't venture onto the streets in Thailand at the time of Songkran. No amount of protesting will save you from a thorough soaking.

Opposite: The tradition of honouring parents by ceremonially washing their feet is still practised, but Songkran is increasingly a festival for the young and is an excuse to get wet and have fun.

Above: In Bangkok and Chiang Mai, the location of two of the biggest Songkran celebrations, the streets fill with revellers.

Right: Nobody is spared a good drenching, however dangerous.

Performing Arts & Sports

Thai Dance

Graceful and enchanting, traditional Thai dance is one of the must-see experiences of any visit to Thailand. The ancient performance art has origins that can be dated to 1431. It includes six distinct forms; the *khon*, a formal masked dance drama that was originally performed for the royal courts and plays out the traditional epic fable of the Ramakien; *lakhon* encompasses several types of dance dramas; *likhe*, a partly improvized folk play with elements of dance, comedy, music and melodrama; *manohra*, the southern Thai version of *likhe*; *nang* or shadow plays; and *hun luang* or puppet theatre.

Beat of a Nation

Thai music ranges from highly stylized classical to *mor lam*, the up-tempo sound of Issan. Although influenced by Khmer and Indian musical traditions, Thai classical music has developed its own distinctive sound. A Thai classical ensemble is called a *piphat* and includes two xylophones, an oboe, barrel drums and two sets of gongs.

Below: The thriving tourist industry has ensured the survival of traditional dance and cultural performances are common in hotels and restaurants.

Left: 'Muay Thai' is a full-on contact sport and boxers are free to use fists, feet and knees to try to beat their opponent.

Below: A good place to watch 'takraw' being played in Bangkok is Benjasiri Park, also known as Queen's Park, sandwiched between the Emporium shopping centre and the Queen's Park Imperial Hotel. Teams play every evening from about 5 p.m.

Muay Thai

Muay Thai, or Thai boxing, is the undisputed national sport of Thailand. The origins of *muay Thai* are said to be on the battlefields of ancient Siam where it was used as a close combat technique by soldiers in battle.

The full-on, close contact nature of *muay Thai* means that it is more brutal than conventional boxing but it is also more exciting for boxing fans to watch. Each bout of *muay Thai* begins with a ritual performed in the ring by both contestants. Known as *wai kru* or *ram muay*, the dance-like ceremony dates back centuries and is intended to honour the boxer's trainer, and pay respect to the spirits.

Bangkok's most well-known venue for *muay Thai* is Lumpini Stadium on Rama IV Road. Established in 1956, it is one of seven major boxing stadiums in the country where bouts are held several nights each week. Ratchadamnern Boxing Stadium on Ratchadamnern Nok Avenue in Bangkok is another popular venue.

Takraw

Takraw is an incredibly athletic sport – a kind of full-on, no-holds-barred volleyball. After work, groups of office workers gather to knock around a rattan ball using their head, hands, arms and feet. Watching them leap in the air and kick the ball over a net with pin-point accuracy is extremely entertaining.

Arts & Crafts

Thailand has come to be regarded as one of Asia's great shopping destinations, attracting visitors from around the globe. The country is excellent for sourcing quality interior décor products, furniture, jewellery, clothing and much more. The government OTOP initiative (One Tambon, One Product) has served to highlight the wonderful diversity of crafts on offer across the country.

Glazed Expressions

Thailand has a long and rich tradition of producing high quality ceramics. From the sophisticated glazed wares of Sukhothai produced for export as early as the 12th century to simple earthenware pots for domestic use and the exquisite green glazed celadon, the tradition continues. The majority of ceramics are produced in factories in the northern towns of Chiang Mai and Lampang but can be purchased all over the country.

Top: The village of Bor Sang on the outskirts of Chiang Mai is famous for making traditional 'saa' paper umbrellas.

Above: Artists in Chiang Mai and the northeast make replicas of temple carvings using clay. After they have been left to weather, they look centuries old.

Left: The northern city of Chiang Mai is renowned for ceramics where many factories produce traditional celadon and highly decorated pots.

Left: Painstakingly weaving an intricately patterned length of silk requires great skill.

Below: Silversmiths in Chiang Mai are concentrated in the Wualai Road area of the city where there are many workshops producing exquisite designs. Silver is also sold in the city's Night Bazaar.

Bottom: 'Saa' paper umbrellas are still made and decorated completely by hand.

Silken Threads

Thailand is known as the major producer of high quality silk. The finest work is hand-woven in the villages of the northeast. On a typical hand-operated loom a skilled weaver can produce about four metres (13 ft) of silk a day. Thai silk is available in shops and markets across the country.

Silverware

The majority of Thailand's best silverware is produced in Chiang Mai. Here you will find delicately patterned silverware bowls and jewellery from Thailand, Laos and Burma along with antique and modern hill tribe jewellery.

'Saa' Paper & Umbrellas

Mulberry paper or *saa* paper, as it is known locally, has been produced in Thailand for almost 700 years. Traditionally, *saa* paper is used for Buddhist scripts, temple decor, umbrellas, fans and kites.

Chapter 2: Bangkok

Bangkok, or *Krung Thep* as it is known to locals, is all things to all people. Here, the modern world collides with deep-rooted culture and traditions. Rise early and witness Buddhist monks collecting alms from local shopkeepers, or find the young and old in quiet contemplation within the grounds of a secluded temple before heading to school or work. The morning rush sees workers crossing the mighty Chao Phraya in river taxis, commuting by bus, or travelling above the city streets in the air-conditioned comfort of the SkyTrain to avoid nightmarish traffic congestion. A city of many charms, even those who are not easily seduced end up falling for Bangkok.

Below: *In the past few years the quality of life in Bangkok has improved immensely. Gone are the days when visitors spent a night in the city and moved on. Bangkok is now a destination in its own right.*

Below: *Bangkok's layout and architectural style often leave visitors bemused but there are some truly impressive structures such as Bhumibol Bridge on Rama III Road.*

Above: Bangkok's skyline is constantly evolving. In recent years a series of elevated walkways linking SkyTrain stations with shopping malls and office blocks has been constructed.

Above: The SkyTrain carries commuters above the congestion, making the city a breeze to get around. There is also an efficient underground system called the MRT.

Left: The eight-lane Sathorn Road passes through the heart of Bangkok's financial district.

This page: Thailand has some of the most impressive temples in Southeast Asia. The glorious Grand Palace and the Temple of the Emerald Buddha, known as Wat Phra Kaew, is one of Bangkok's most visited attractions. Completed in 1784, the temple compound has over 100 buildings, golden spires and glittering mosaics. The main building houses a 70-cm (27^1/$_2$-in) tall Emerald Buddha.

Opposite page: Wat Arun, or the Temple of the Dawn, is situated on the banks of the Chao Phraya River and can be reached by boat. The 79-m (259-ft) pagoda is decorated with fragments of porcelain plates and bowls. The temple is particularly beautiful at sunset or when viewed from the deck of an evening rivercruise boat.

Right: Wat Pho, or Wat Phra Chetuphon as it is also known, is famous for a huge Reclining Buddha. The 46-m (151-ft) long and 15-m (49-ft) high figure was constructed in 1832. The Buddha is in the position of passing into nirvana. The enormous feet feature mother-of-pearl inlay decoration showing the 108 auspicious characteristics of Buddha.

Above: Situated on an 8-hectare (20-acre) site, Wat Pho is also one of the largest in Bangkok. Wat Pho is also a centre for the teaching of traditional Thai medicine and massage.

Right: The temple has 95 'chedis' of varying sizes, the largest of which were built to commemorate the first four kings of the Chakri dynasty.

Left: The Giant Swing, or Sao Ching Chor, is a distinctive Bangkok landmark. Once used in Brahmanic ceremonies long since discontinued, the original swing was replaced in 2007 to honour the King of Thailand. Nearby shops around Bamrung Muang Road sell Buddha images and religious supplies making it a fascinating area to explore.

Above: Wat Suthat is renowned for 19th-century murals and a beautiful 13th-century 8-metre (26-ft) tall bronze Buddha image with the ashes of King Rama VIII in its base. In the cloisters there is also an unusual black Buddha image.

Left: Wat Benchamabophit, also known as the Marble Temple, is unusual in that it is one of the few temples in Thailand to feature western-style stained glass windows with Buddhist imagery. It also has beautiful old monks' quarters.

Above: Bangkok's Chinatown is a bustling district of crowded alleyways, restaurants, gold shops and temples. During the cooler months visitors may also be lucky enough to see an outdoor performance of a traditional Chinese opera.

Right: If you think Bangkok always moves at full speed, rise early and head along to Lumpini Park and watch the Chinese locals exercising or practising their controlled 'tai chi' moves in the shade.

Above: Jim Thompson House is the beautiful former home of the late American silk trader. The house – now a museum – consists of several traditional teak houses brought together to make one splendid home.

Left: Vimanmek Teak Palace is the world's largest teak building. It was originally constructed for King Rama V in 1868 as a summer palace on the island of Koh Si Chang but relocated to the current site in 1910.

Chapter 3: The Central Plains

A network of rivers flowing down from the north feed into the 24 provinces that make up the central plains; a flat and fertile region known as the 'rice bowl' of the country. The region also has many manmade waterways that are used for irrigating the fields and navigating the vast area.

Ayutthaya

Ayutthaya is one of the most culturally and historically interesting towns within easy reach of Bangkok. The ancient ruins have been encroached upon by the new town, creating an interesting blend of ancient and modern.

Above: The 'chedi' at Wat Yai Chai Mongkhon is surrounded by lines of Buddha images draped in saffron robes. The temple was built at the request of King U Thong in the 14th century.

Below: Wat Yai Chai Mongkhon is one of the most impressive 'chedis' within the Ayutthaya Historical Park. Visitors to the site can climb up the steps and enjoy fabulous views from the base of the central 'chedi'.

These pages: The combined ancient monuments of Ayutthaya were awarded UNESCO World Heritage status in 1991. Accessible by rail, river and road, Thailand's former capital was once praised by foreign emissaries as the finest city they had ever seen. The three pagodas of Wat Phra Si Sanphet (bottom left) are a highlight of a visit to Ayutthaya. Two were originally built on the orders of King Ramathibodi II in honour of his father, King Borommatrailokanat and his brother King Borommarachathirat III. The third one houses his own remains.

Chapter 4: The Eastern Seaboard

The eastern region of Thailand comprises the provinces of Chonburi, Rayong, Trat, Chanthaburi, Chachoengsao and Prachinburi. The area is extremely varied and includes industrial zones in Chonburi, and the beach resort city of Pattaya, along with beautiful countryside.

Pattaya

Set beside a glorious sweeping bay and a white sand beach, Pattaya is a favourite destination for those wishing to flee Bangkok at weekends and for long-haul travellers seeking fun in the sun. At night, Pattaya comes alive. The city is transformed from a quiet town into a noisy and neon-lit warren of bars and massage parlours.

Above: In the 1970s, Pattaya was nothing more than a small fishing village. Today it is a booming city known as the party capital of Thailand. In recent years, the Tourist Authority of Thailand has tried to clean up Pattaya's image, but without conspicuous success.

Left: Those seeking to get away from the crowded beaches of Pattaya and its rowdy nightlife can take a trip to nearby Koh Lam.

This page: Although Pattaya is renowned for its go-go bars and discos, there are many other attractions in the area including fishing villages and fresh seafood markets, a vineyard and theme parks. A big attraction for Buddhists is Khao Chi Chan, a cliff face with Thailand's largest Buddha image. Located a short distance from Pattaya, the 109-m (358-ft) tall and 70-m (230-ft) wide image was created in 1996 to honour King Bhumibol The outline of the Buddha in a seated position was etched into the cliff using a laser before golden tiles were applied.

Chapter 5: Western Thailand

Western Thailand encompasses many interesting provinces, some of which are a comfortable driving distance from Bangkok. Highlights include Prachuap Khirikhan and the royal resort town of Hua Hin, and Kanchanaburi, the location of the infamous bridge over the River Kwai built by POWs in the Second World War.

Much of western Thailand is a flat and fertile expanse of land covered with fruit trees and coconut palm plantations and is irrigated by an extensive network of canals. Samut Songkhram Province is well irrigated and as a result intensely agricultural. The area is renowned for coconut palms, guava, lychees and in recent years a vineyard. Salt is processed in a series of man-made lakes and there are also several floating markets in the area.

Above: Rise early in the morning and you'll see monks walking down the beach at Hua Hin to collect alms from locals and hotel guests.

Left: There are several floating markets in the western region and within easy driving distance of Bangkok. Nowadays they function purely as a tourist attraction.

Above: The provinces of Samut Sakhorn and Samut Songkhram are famous for salt fields. Sea water is directed into large shallow ponds where it evaporates leaving pure salt crystals.

Right: Hua Hin is the location of one of the region's most celebrated and historic hotels. Formerly the Railway Hotel and now the Sofitel Hua Hin, it was here that scenes from 'The Killing Fields' were filmed.

Hua Hin

As the location of the King of Thailand's summer palace, Hua Hin had always found favour with wealthy Bangkok Thais long before it was discovered by Western tourists. Today, it is not just big city Thais slipping away for a weekend of clean air and fresh seafood who visit the town. Hua Hin is now squarely on the map as a premier holiday destination and is attracting visitors from around the world. Hua Hin is an excellent family destination, a paradise for golfers and an idyllic place for retirees wishing to escape the dark and cold European winters.

Below: Hua Hin Hills Vineyard produces some of Thailand's better quality vintages, namely Monsoon Valley Wine. Visitors can enjoy wine tasting in the restaurant and elephant rides through the vines.

Above right: The beachfront is lined with seafood restaurants and international five star resorts.

Right: The beautiful railway station is one of the oldest, best-preserved examples in Thailand.

Kanchanaburi & the River Kwai

Bordering Myanmar, Kanchanaburi Province is home to the infamous bridge over the River Kwai and the haunting museum dedicated to the memory of those who perished constructing the Death Railway for the Japanese during the Second World War. It is hard to reconcile the brutality and suffering endured here with the region's beauty, yet it is heartening to see just how many people travel from around the world to pay their respects.

Top right: Two well-tended cemeteries in the centre of Kanchanaburi are the last resting place of the thousands of soldiers who lost their lives in the Second World War.

Above: Although this is not the original bridge over the River Kwai, the structure that now spans the river is lit up every night and creates a beautiful, if thought-provoking, sight.

Above: Visitors to Kanchanaburi can travel by train through beautiful countryside to the Hellfire Pass Memorial Museum, an honourable tribute to the war dead.

Chapter 6: Northeast Thailand

The northeast of Thailand consists of 18 culturally diverse provinces collectively known locally as Issan. Culturally rich and populated by fun-loving, resilient and hard-working people, Issan is one of the country's most fascinating regions but also the least visited. With only two per cent of tourists visiting the northeast, many travellers to Thailand are missing out on a beautiful and distinctive part of the kingdom.

Below left: A street-side vendor sells bundles of lemongrass, ginger, coriander and other essentials of Thai cuisine.

Khorat

Khorat, also known as Nakhon Ratchasima, is the gateway to Issan and is the northeast's largest city. Although the province is largely rural and undeveloped, the city itself has benefited from commercial investment and attracted migrants from towns and villages across the northeast. The surrounding districts have much to offer visitors, including Phimai, one of Thailand's most impressive ancient temples.

Left: The old town of Khorat was once enclosed by a defensive wall. Only small sections remain. During the 14th century, Khorat and nearby Phimai were under the rule of the Khmer empire.

Above: Regional Issan food is loved all over Thailand. Famous dishes include the spicy papaya salad, 'som tam', and grilled chicken or 'gai yang'. In the northeast, sticky rice is preferred to steamed rice.

Left: Although hypermarkets are changing shopping habits in Thailand, morning markets in Khorat are extremely popular. Locals come each day to buy freshly cooked food for their breakfast as well as fresh vegetables, fish and meat.

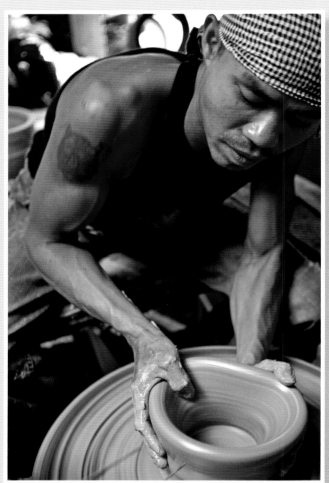

This page: A shrine in front of Khorat's western gate honours Thao Suranaree, a heroine who is said to have helped defeat Lao invaders by getting them drunk (above left). A festival is held to celebrate the occasion every March. In Khorat, and many other rural towns, samlors, three-wheeled bicycles, are still used to transport produce and people (below).

Located 15 km (9 miles) from Khorat, the town of Dan Kwien is known for producing earthenware pottery (above right). Although pots have been produced in the area since the 15th century, today the work is anything but traditional. Dozens of stalls line the road selling all kinds of decorative items for the home.

Phimai Temple

Issan is scattered with remarkable ruins that chart its fascinating history. Of the many ancient temple sites, the most spectacular is Phimai, not far from the booming town of Khorat. Easily reached from Khorat by bus, the ruins of Phimai are an essential part of any itinerary for the northeast. The temple structure is actually Khmer and predates Angkor in Cambodia. During the glory days of the Angkor Empire, Phimai was directly connected by road to Angkor.

This page: During the Khmer period, Prasat Hin Phimai was an important temple. Construction is believed to have been carried out in the 10th century under the orders of the Khmer King Suryavarman I. The ancient monument is laid out in a rectangle measuring 565 by 1,030 m (1,854 by 3,379 ft) and is surrounded by a moat. The structure is the largest and arguably the most impressive stone edifice in all Thailand. The outer walls and the lintels of the tower are decorated with exquisite carvings depicting episodes from the Ramayana.

Buriram

Buriram is one of Thailand's larger provinces and a former centre of Khmer culture. A highlight of any visit to this area is Phanom Rung Historical Park, a magnificent Khmer site dating back over 1,000 years to the Angkor period. The impressive stone ruins of Phanom Rung are the finest example of Khmer monuments in Thailand.

Ubon Ratchathani

In the southeast of Issan the town of Ubon Ratchathani marks the start of the rainy season retreat with Thailand's largest and most spectacular candle festival. The event includes a candlelit procession of intricately carved beeswax candles, many of which are several metres tall, and commemorates Buddha's first sermon after attaining enlightenment more than 2,500 years ago.

Above: Situated on the site of an extinct volcano, Phanom Rung was originally a religious site for Hindu worship but later became an important Buddhist temple. Further additions were made during the 15th–18th centuries. Recently the ancient temple has benefited from significant restoration work carried out by Thailand's Fine Arts Department.

North of Issan

The northern reaches of Issan should not be overlooked by travellers. In Nong Khai visitors can enjoy evenings dining beside the Mekong River and cross into neighbouring Laos via the Friendship Bridge. There's also the stunning Sala Kaew Ku Buddha Park to explore. Further west in Loei, one of Thailand's least visited but most beautiful provinces, attractions include the Phu Kradeung National Park. During the cool season, Thais come to climb Phu Kradeung Mountain and enjoy the views and pleasant climate.

Above: Just outside Nong Khai, the impressive Thai-Lao Friendship Bridge opened in 1994. Spanning 1,170 m (3,840 ft) across the Mekong River, the bridge now includes the first rail link between Thailand and Laos. The bridge was also instrumental in transforming Nong Khai from a sleepy and seldom visited riverside town into a popular travellers' stopover with many floating restaurants and bars.

Below: Created in 1978 by the shaman, Bounleua Sulilat who fled Laos during the country's political upheaval, the enormous sculptures in Sala Kaew Ku Buddha Park are an intriguing mix of Hindu and Buddhist imagery. Before coming to Thailand, Bounleua had also built the Xieng Kuan Buddha Park outside Vientiane.

Chapter 7: Northern Thailand

The north of Thailand is a beautiful, mountainous, forest-covered region bordering Myanmar and Laos. It consists of 18 provinces including Chiang Mai, Chiang Rai, Nan and Mae Hong Son. Farming flourishes in the fertile northern valleys and the area produces much of Thailand's annual crops of fruits and vegetables.

Many people travel to Chiang Mai and the north for trekking in the mountains. The area is populated by six major hill tribes, the Karen, Hmong, Lahu, Yao, Akha and Lisu. Each tribe has distinctive clothing, customs and language. Popular attractions also include elephant camps, orchid farms and stunning temples.

Below: Northern Thailand's rolling hills and beautiful scenery attract nature lovers and cultural travellers. A network of excellent roads winds through the hills and a jeep or motorcycle hired in Chiang Mai offer excellent ways to explore the region. The cool season months of November to February are the best time to visit the north when the mornings and evenings are pleasantly chilly, but the afternoons warm.

Left: There are several elephant camps around Chiang Mai, the best of which is the award-winning Elephant Nature Park in Mae Taeng district. The founder, Lek Chailert, was named 'Asian Hero of the Year' by 'Time' magazine. The park endeavours to let the elephants live as natural a life as possible.

Above: Orchids flourish in the highlands of northern Thailand. There are many farms selling cultivated orchids in the Mae Rim district of Chiang Mai

Sukhothai & Baan Koh Noi

Home to magnificent temples, ruins and monuments, the Sukhothai Historical Park is a UNESCO World Heritage Site and draws thousands of visitors every year. The historical park is divided into five zones that can be explored by bicycle. The Ramkhamhaeng National Museum within the site gives visitors an interesting historical perspective and is a good starting point before exploring the park. Nearby Baan Koh Noi receives fewer visitors, but is also home to impressive temple ruins.

Below: Sukhothai is located 427 km (265 miles) north of Bangkok and 300 km (186 miles) south of Chiang Mai. In November it is also the site of the biggest Loy Kratong festival.

Right: The hand of the huge Buddha image at Wat Si Chum in Sukhothai is covered with gold leaf rubbed onto the fingers by the thousands of worshippers who pray before it.

Left: Less visited than Sukhothai, but nevertheless well worth seeing, are the temple ruins at Baan Koh Noi. An hour's drive from Sukhothai, the site has many impressive temples, an interesting museum and many ancient kilns where high quality pottery was produced.

Below: Approaching Wat Si Chum along the pathway, the face of the enormous Buddha is first glimpsed through an opening in the front wall. The temple is located outside the walls of the old city at the northwest corner.

Lampang

Legend has it that the northern town of Lampang was once called Kuk Kutta Nakorn, meaning 'city of the white cockerel'. Today, the town is famous for ceramics with a distinctive chicken motif, and as being the only town in Thailand with horse-drawn carriages.

This page: *The lovely northern town of Lampang should not be overlooked. It has much of interest to captivate visitors for several days. The most famous temple in the area is Wat Phra That Lampang Luang which features a 45-m (148-ft) 'chedi' (above left). In the reign of King Rama VI the first railway line from Bangkok to the north of Thailand was completed and on 1 April 1916 Lampang station opened. One of the early steam trains still stands outside the station. Today, travellers can alight at Lampang and explore the town before heading further north to Chiang Mai. Years ago, Chinese settlers established ceramics workshops producing noodle bowls. Today, Lampang is the centre of Thailand's ceramics industry with many factories located on the outskirts of town.*

Chiang Mai

Chiang Mai is the largest city in the north and is a provincial capital. Chiang Mai's tree-lined streets, stunning temples, historic sites, bustling markets and varied nightlife make it one of the nicest cities in Thailand to visit.

This page: The northern provincial capital, once a sleepy backpacker haven, has expanded rapidly in recent years. Yet despite the obvious challenges associated with rapid development, Chiang Mai remains a city of character and a province of undeniable beauty. The distinctive Lanna culture and the easygoing charm of the northern people are huge natural assets. The city wins the hearts of all who visit. Attractions include Doi Suthep, a 1,600-m (5,249-ft) peak overlooking Chiang Mai and the site of the famous temple Wat Phra That Doi Suthep. Another famous temple, Wat Chedi Luang, was constructed in the 15th century but an earthquake in 1545 destroyed the massive 'chedi'. Even what remains today is a remarkable sight. The Ping River flows through the centre of Chiang Mai. Visitors can enjoy trips down the river and dinner cruises in the evening when the air is cooler. Alternatively evenings can be spent dining in riverside restaurants or shopping for unique local crafts in the markets.

Chiang Rai

Known as the 'Gateway to the Golden Triangle', the city of Chiang Rai lies in a fertile valley 180 km (112 miles) north of Chiang Mai. The town has a less commercial feel than Chiang Mai and consequently a more relaxed atmosphere. Mountainous and bordered by the mighty Mekong River, Chiang Rai Province is a playground for those seeking adventure and stunning scenery.

This page: Wat Rong Khun is one of Chiang Rai's most spectacular attractions. This beautiful temple is the ongoing work of the renowned Thai artist, Chalermchai Kositpipat, and skilfully blends traditional Buddhist art with modern concepts. The unique building is entirely white and decorated with thousands of pieces of mirrored glass. Inside, it contains murals and paintings with some very surprising imagery. Outside, a hole with dozens of hands reaching upwards for help is the artist's interpretation of hell. The temple also includes artworks that warn about the dangers of smoking and drinking. Located 13 km (8 miles) from Chiang Rai, Wat Rong Khun is particularly impressive when visited on the night of a full moon.

This page: Two other notable attractions in Chiang Rai are Rai Mae Fah Luang and Black House. Rai Mae Fah Luang includes an outstanding botanical garden and the Mae Fah Luang Art and Cultural Park, home to the royal collection of Lanna art, while Black House (right) is the wonderfully eccentric vision of celebrated Thai artist, Tawan Datchanee. The expansive estate features many unusual buildings and sculptures (above).

Mae Sai

A bustling town on the Thai-Myanmar border, Mae Sai attracts visitors wishing to shop in the colourful market and cross into the Burmese town of Tachilek for a day.

Below: Mae Sai is surrounded by mountains and hill tribe villagers can often be seen in the local market. The many Burmese living and working in the area add a unique colour and character to the town.

Left: Much of the street food in Mae Sai is regional Burmese cuisine, such as spicy Shan-style noodle dishes.

Right: The markets and shops are full of arts and crafts from Myanmar, such as these handmade puppets.

Golden Triangle

Once renowned for opium production, the Golden Triangle, known locally as Sop Ruak, is now a major tourist destination. Today's legal vice is gambling and here, where the borders of Laos, Myanmar and Thailand converge, many cross into the neighbouring countries to try their luck at the tables of the casinos.

This page: Nine kilometres (5¹/2 miles) from the historic town of Chiang Saen and at the confluence of the Mekong and Ruak Rivers, the Golden Triangle is an area of outstanding natural beauty. At a local temple, visitors can enjoy views over Laos and Myanmar. Nearby, the Hall of Opium recounts the Golden Triangle's infamous past and also serves as a drug education centre. The fascinating museum also includes an information centre for research and education on opium, opiates and other narcotics. The museum is one of the best in Thailand and has received several awards. The area is home to many hill tribes, particularly Akha (shown here) who used to be involved in opium production. Today they make a living from growing crops such as sweetcorn, pineapple and cabbage or selling their handicrafts.

Doi Mae Salong

Doi Mae Salong is a historic village situated in a beautiful mountain setting north of Chiang Rai. With an elevation of 1,800 m (5,905 ft) , a trip to the area ensures breathtaking panoramic views and dramatic sunsets. The air is refreshing all year round and from November until February it can be quite cold. Doi Mae Salong mountain range is renowned for its tea plantations cultivated by local hill tribes.

Top right: The road from Chiang Rai winds through stunning countryside, eventually arriving at the tea plantations.

Above: There are many Akha and Lisu settlements in the area whose inhabitants work in the tea plantations.

Left: Wat Acha Tong, or the Temple of the Golden Horse, was established by an ex-Thai boxer turned Buddhist monk to help care for orphans. The monks are renowned for collecting alms on horseback.

Mae Hong Son

The provincial capital of Mae Hong Son is a scenic and vibrant town and a centre for tourists seeking adventure in the surrounding mountains. The townspeople are predominately Shan, also referred to as Thai Yai, and local temple architecture shows the strong influence they have exerted over the region in the past. Hill tribe people scattered throughout the mountains and frequently seen in the town's markets include Karen, Lisu, Lahu and Musoe. Mae Hong Son is one of the country's premier destinations for trekking and soft adventure.

This page: The road from Chiang Mai to Mae Hong Son and onward to Mae Sariang is nothing short of spectacular, boasting hundreds of hairpin bends as it winds through the thrilling mountainous terrain. It is understandably popular with adventure motorcyclists and 4-wheel-drive enthusiasts who also take advantage of the numerous dirt trails that lead off into more remote areas. The rewards are great; Mae Hong Son has a unique character, people and cuisine that make it one of Thailand's most fascinating regions.

Chapter 8: Southern Thailand, Islands and Beaches

The south of Thailand encompasses many of Thailand's most popular holiday destinations including Phuket, Thailand's largest island.

Phuket

Phuket (pronounced *pooket*) is Thailand's largest island (930 km²/360 sq miles – about the size of Singapore) and is known as the Pearl of the Andaman. The interior of Phuket is tree-covered and hilly with land rising to over 500 m (1,640 ft). In the lowland areas there are many rubber and coconut plantations, once an important occupation for islanders but now increasing sidelined by tourism.

This page: *Famous beaches include Kata Beach, one of the most beautiful in Phuket. The fabulous stretch of sand is washed by crystal clear waters and lined with palm trees. Surin Beach occupies a curved bay below the foothills north of Kamala. The area is dotted with some of Phuket's most prestigious resorts and high-end boutiques. This has given the quiet and beautiful beach an air of exclusivity – a world away from brash Patong. With a large marina on the island, Phuket attracts members of the international yachting fraternity and also plays host to a huge annual regatta.*

Right: A Buddha image in a recess of the outer wall at Wat Chalong. Dedicated to two venerable monks, this is considered to be Phuket's most important temple. In 1876 when Chinese tin miners on the island rebelled, it is believed that they sought sanctuary in Wat Chalong.

Phuket Town

Phuket Town is the island's commercial centre and is situated to the southeast of the island. Despite the recent boom in modern development, the town is still home to some splendid Sino-Portuguese architecture.

Below: *The historic Phuket Town is a charming area to explore. Wander down the Dibuk, Thalang, Phang Nga, Yaowarat and Krabi roads to discover Phuket's past.*

Right: *Phuket has some of Thailand's finest examples of period architecture but it is only in recent years that this has started to be valued as a local asset. Even so, many buildings are still in need of protection and restoration.*

Patong

Patong is Phuket's most famous and most developed beach. For some it is the heart and soul of a holiday in Phuket, for others a tourist trap that is best avoided. The 3-km (2-mile) long stretch of sand is lined with shops, bars and good seafood restaurants, and also offers great leisure activities including windsurfing and kite surfing, sailing, swimming and sunbathing. Patong also has a reputation as the centre of Phuket's vibrant nightlife. It is here that you will find most of the rowdy pubs, clubs and go-go bars.

This page: Of the six beach districts of Phuket that offer evening entertainment, Patong is by far the liveliest. By day, the shoreline buzzes with the sound of jet skis and the sky is filled with paragliders towed by speedboats. At night, Bangla Road and Soi Sunset are packed with bars and western-style nightclubs while Soi Sea Dragon is home to some raunchy entertainment and the majority of the go-go bars. This is definitely not the destination for those in search of a quiet beach holiday, Thai culture or authentic cuisine.

Nai Yang

Nai Yang is located in the north of Phuket, just a short drive from the airport. Despite this, it is not troubled by aircraft noise. In fact, Nai Yang is the ideal place for a quiet and relaxing getaway. The lovely curving bay has a wide stretch of sand and is lapped by trees and edged with small beachfront restaurants.

Right: Nai Yang is known for fabulous sunsets. The tree-lined beach has many small restaurants in which to enjoy a cool beer with Thai food as the sun sinks into the Andaman Sea.

Below: Nai Yang has so far escaped the uncontrolled development that has affected many other beach resorts. The perfect choice for families and romantics seeking a peaceful retreat, it brings to mind the Phuket of 20 years ago.

Above: Even at the peak seaon, Nai Yang is one of Phuket's quietest beaches. In the low season months of May to September, you can almost have the beach to yourself.

Below: Just a short drive from Nai Yang Beach, the Blue Canyon Country Club features two award-winning 18-hole courses, the Canyon and the Lakes. Open to non-members, the course attracts golfers from Europe, Japan and Korea.

Phang Nga

Phang Nga Province is blessed with turquoise waters and striking rock formations. As the location of the famous James Bond island in *The Man With The Golden Gun*, it is also one of the most recognizable and most visited destinations in Thailand. Day trips by boat are available from Phuket.

Right: The location for the movie, 'The Man with the Golden Gun', the distinctive rock formation called Khao Tapoo, or Nail Island, is now simply referred to as James Bond Island.

Opposite: Long-tail boats wait to ferry visitors to James Bond Island. The downside of the island's fame is that tourists come here in their thousands and a once deserted beach heaves with souvenir sellers.

Below: Ao Phang Nga National Park covers an area of 400 km² (154 sq miles) and protects the largest area of primary mangrove forest remaining in Thailand. It encompasses more than 42 large and small islands.

Koh Samui

Once a haven for backpackers, Koh Samui is now one of Thailand's most popular travel destinations. Large numbers of visitors come to enjoy an idyllic climate, white sand beaches, water sports and a vibrant nightlife. Situated 700 km (435 miles) south of Bangkok but only an hour and a half by air, the island is easy to reach. The 250-square kilometre (97-square mile) island is at the edge of the Ang Tong National Marine Park which includes 80 other islands, only six of which are inhabited.

Opposite above: Koh Hong or Room Island in Krabi takes its name from the eroded caves and lake which can be reached through a narrow opening from the sea. Fearless locals can also be seen in the caves climbing bamboo ladders to collect swallows' nests for birds' nest soup.

Below: The biggest and busiest beach on Koh Samui is Chaweng Beach, on the eastern side of the island. The majority of the island's hotels, bars and restaurants are clustered around Chaweng and it is also the centre of the busiest nightlife.

Krabi

Idyllic islands and beaches, clear waters, tropical rainforest and protected national parks have gained Krabi a well-deserved reputation as one of the world's most beautiful destinations. Around the island of Phi Phi Don a wide range of interesting activities including climbing, caving, diving and snorkelling can be enjoyed.

Left: Located one hour from Krabi Town, Koh Hong is popular with day trippers who come to enjoy the powdery sands of Pelay Beach and snorkel in the azure waters which are teeming with tropical fish and coral formations. For the more adventurous, the island's limestone outcrops offer rock climbers over 100 challenging routes.

Getting About

Thailand has an excellent transport infrastructure and is easy to get around, even in rural areas. There are currently six international airports: Suvarnabhumi, Chiang Mai, Chiang Rai, Hat Yai, Koh Samui and Phuket. The gateway airport, Suvarnabhumi is located 30 km (19 miles) east of downtown Bangkok and provides both international and domestic flights. From the airport, the city can be reached by taxi using the expressway or by the new elevated rail link. For taxis, allow one hour to reach the city centre. The train takes 25 minutes and passes through eight stations: Lad Krabang, Thab Chang, Hua Mark, Ramkhamhaeng, City Air Terminal, Makkasan, Rajprarop and Phayathai on the BTS SkyTrain line. Several airlines offer regular domestic flights to a network of local airports.

Opposite: Thais are extremely proud and protective of the ubiquitous tuk-tuk. Noisy, uncomfortable, unbearable in a traffic jam and probably overpriced if you are a tourist, it's a must-try experience on any trip to Thailand!

Below: Hua Lampong Station is Bangkok's main railway station with trains leaving day and night for all four regions.

Other options for travel around the country include trains. Thailand has one of the best railway networks in Southeast Asia and although progress along the aging tracks can be slow, the somewhat sedate pace is one of its great attractions. Hua Lampong Station in central Bangkok, conveniently connected to the MRT underground system, is the hub for all rail travel in Thailand. The network penetrates all regions of the country, passing through some of the most beautiful countryside and pulling into many small, but bustling, stations. As a passenger in the comfortable first, second or third class carriages, you are afforded the opportunity to see a part of the country and a way of life that is completely missed by those who fly. Cheap and convenient, travel by train also allows you the luxury and adventure of being able to jump off anywhere you please along the line. Sleeper cars are also available for overnight travel. From Bangkok, tracks stretch northwards to Chiang Mai and east into Issan, where the line divides at Nakhon Ratchasima, with one line running up to Nong Khai and onward over the Laos border, and the other heading for Ubon Ratchathani. A shorter branch line also runs from Bangkok to the town of Aranya

and beaches. Moving along at an unhurried pace, the comfortable carriages pass through the royal resort of Hua Hin and its beautiful old station and then on to Chumphon, Surat Thani and Hat Yai. From here you can even continue by rail on to Kuala Lumpur and Singapore.

Bus travel in Thailand is extremely popular and cheap. The country's roads are also excellent. The best option – the quickest and the most comfortable – are the VIP coaches. In towns and rural areas, travel options include motorcycle taxis, *songtaews*, an open-back truck with two bench seats, and the ubiquitous tuk-tuk. In more touristy areas, there are many scooter and car hire shops which often prove to be the cheapest and most convenient option.

Phratet on the Thai-Cambodian border. Train enthusiasts and historians can travel west to Kanchanaburi, the site of the famous 'bridge over the River Kwai' and Hellfire Pass, or use the line to travel south to reach Thailand's idyllic islands

Below: *Local buses may be cheap but they stop frequently and lack air-conditioning. VIP buses are a better option.*

Resources

Tourist Police

Bilingual Tourist Police are affiliated with the Tourism Authority of Thailand offices in Bangkok, Phra Nakhon Si Ayutthaya, Pattaya, Kanchanaburi, Nakhon Ratchasima, Udon Thani, Khon Kaen, Chiang Mai, Chiang Rai, Mae Hong Son, Phitsanulok, Nakhon Sawan, Surat Thani, Phuket and Songkhla to provide assistance for visitors.

In the case of an emergency, contact the Tourist Police Centre, Ratchadamnoen Nok Avenue, Bangkok 10200. Tel: 1155 (free 24 hours).

Contacts

The following websites contain useful information for organizing your trip to Thailand.

Tourist Authority of Thailand; www.tatnews.org and www.tourismthailand.org

1 Stop Thailand: www.1stopthailand.com

Amazing Thailand: www.amazing-thailand.com

G-T Rider: www.gt-rider.com

Chiang Mai Thai Cookery School: www.thaicookeryschool.com

National Museums of Thailand: www.nationalmuseums.finearts.go.th

Thailand Guidebook: www.thailandguidebook.com

Thai National Parks: www.dnp.go.th

Airlines

Thai Airways: www.thaiairways.com

Nok Air: www.nokair.com

Nok Mini: www.sga.co.th

Bangkok Airways: www.bangkokair.com

Orient Thai Airlines: www.flyorientthai.com

Solar Air: www.solarair.co.th

Happy Air: www.happyair.co.th

AirAsia: www.airasia.com

References

Phongpaichit, Pasuk and Baker, Chris. 1998. *Thailand's Boom and Bust*. Silkworm Books.

Rough Guide to World Music. 2009. Rough Guides.

Shippen, Mick. 2005. *The Traditional Ceramics of South East Asia*. A&C Black.

Warren, William. 1995. *Arts & Crafts of Thailand*. Thames & Hudson Ltd.

Wyatt, David K. 2004. *Thailand: A Short History*. Yale University Press.

Yen Ho, Alice. 1995. *At the South-East Asian Table*. Oxford University Press.

Acknowledgements

Many thanks to the Princess of Kalasin, Sudarat Ponpangpa, Christian Schlegel at Sofitel Bangkok Silom, Madam Aong at Sheraton Grande Sukhumvit, Bangkok, Tracey Malone, Lillian Woon Carpenter at Dewa Phuket, Paweena Swing at Westin Grande Sukhumvit, Bangkok, Sutassa Vareetip of Accor, Rebecca Lek at Blue Canyon Country Club, Phuket, Hua Hin Hills Vineyard, Phen Bidasak, northern Thailand's best trekking guide and owner of Little Eden Guesthouse in Mae Hong Son Province, Duangkamol Srisukri of Mengrai Kilns in Chiang Mai and David Bowden.

About the Author

Mick Shippen is a freelance writer and photographer. Based in Thailand since 1997, he currently lives in Bangkok. Mick travels extensively throughout Asia conducting research for articles and taking photographs for local and international newspapers and magazines. He is the author of *The Traditional Ceramics of South East Asia*, as well as a contributing writer for the books *To Asia with Love*, *To Myanmar with Love* and *To Thailand with Love*. His images can been viewed at www.mickshippen.com.

Index

For Tem

Published and Distributed in Thailand by Asia Books Co., Ltd.
Berli Jucker House, 14th Floor, 99 Soi Rubia, Sukhumvit 42 Road, Phrakanong, Klongtoey, Bangkok 10110, Thailand
Tel: (66) 2-715-9000; Fax: (66) 2-715-9197; Email: information@asiabooks.com; www.asiabooks.com

This edition first published in 2013 by John Beaufoy Publishing,
11 Blenheim Court, 316 Woodstock Road, Oxford OX2 7NS, England
www.johnbeaufoy.com

10 9 8 7 6 5 4 3 2

Great care has been taken to maintain the accuracy of the information contained in this work.
However, neither the publishers nor the author can be held responsible for any consequences
arising from the use of the information contained therein.

ISBN 978-1-906780-53-1 (paperback)
ISBN 978-1-906780-67-8 (hardback)

Edited, designed and typeset by Stonecastle Graphics
Cartography by William Smuts
Project management by Rosemary Wilkinson

Printed and bound in Malaysia by Tien Wah Press (Pte) Ltd.

Cover captions and credits:
Back cover (left to right): *A bridge in Wat Benchamabophit, also known as the Marble Temple, Bangkok*,
© Mick Shippen; *Wat Rong Khun, the unique white temple at Chiang Rai*, © Mick Shippen; *Chillies, an essential
ingredient of Thai cuisine*, © Mick Shippen; *Gilded by worshippers, the hand of a huge Buddha image at Wat Si
Chum in Sukhothai*, © Mick Shippen.
Front cover top (left to right): *A temple guardian at the Grand Palace, Bangkok*, © Shutterstock.com/Bryan Busovicki;
Long tailboats by the shore at Hong Island, Krabi, Shutterstock.com/Juriah Mosin; *The Golden Tower of the Grand
Palace, Bangkok*, © Shutterstock.com/ZQFotography; *A floating market in western Thailand*, © Shutterstock.com/
Amy Nichole Harris
Front cover (centre): *Terraced rice fields in northern Thailand*, © Shutterstock.com/platongkoh
Front cover (bottom): *An elephant silhouetted by the sunset near Ayutthaya*, © Shutterstock.com/tanatat